PYGMALION

PYGMALION

by
George Bernard Shaw

Adapted by
Nicole Vittiglio

Illustrated by
Brian Bartle and Tim Davis

Modern Publishing
A Division of Kappa Books Publishers, LLC.

Cover art by Marcel Laverdet

Contents

CHAPTER 1

A Poor Flower Girl

On a cool summer night in Covent Garden, a heavy rain began to beat down. Pedestrians were frantically running into the market and seeking shelter under the entrance to St. Paul's Church. Crowds were beginning to gather. It was close to midnight.

Among the soaking wet crowd were a lady and her daughter, both dressed in fancy evening gowns. They peered out gloomily at the heavy downpour from behind the pillars.

"What in the world can Freddy possibly be doing?" the daughter wondered. "I'm thoroughly chilled, and he's been gone for nearly twenty minutes!"

"He hasn't been gone for that long," the mother replied. "He should have been able to get us a cab by now."

A man standing near them said, "He won't be able to get a cab for at least another fifteen minutes. That's when they come back from dropping off their theater fares."

"If Freddy had a bit of sense, he would have hailed one at the theater door," said the daughter miserably.

"The poor boy is trying his best," the mother said.

"Other people got cabs," the daughter replied. "Why couldn't Freddy?"

Suddenly Freddy came running in from the rain. He was also wearing evening clothes, which were soaking wet around the ankles.

"Well, where is our cab?" the daughter asked Freddy.

"There is not a cab to be had in all of London," Freddy answered.

"There must be one," the mother said. "You can't possibly have tried everywhere."

"Do you want us to go get one ourselves?" the daughter asked.

"I tell you that all of the cabs are taken," Freddy explained. "Since the rain was so sudden, everyone had to take a cab."

"You're helpless, Freddy," the mother said. "Now go out and don't come back until you've found one!"

"But I shall just wind up getting soaked for no reason," Freddy argued.

"What about us?" the daughter asked. "We're cold, you selfish pig!"

"Very well," said Freddy, giving in.

As he opened his umbrella and started to dash off, he collided with a girl selling flowers. She was rushing in from the rain. He knocked her basket right out of her hands, and her flowers went flying all over the ground.

Just then a loud clap of thunder boomed, and lightning flashed across the sky.

"Watch where you're gowin,' Freddy," the flower girl said.

"I'm sorry," said Freddy. He rushed off without stopping to help her.

"There's manners fo' yer," the flower girl muttered. "Two banches of voylets ruined!" The flower girl sat on the base of one of the pillars and started to gather up some of the flowers that had been crushed in the mud. She was about twenty years old and wore a black straw hat that was covered in dust and soot. Her hair needed washing. Her coat, brown dress, apron, and boots were very worn and old. She was just as pretty as any of the ladies that surrounded her, but much less stylish and much more dirty.

"Excuse me, but how do you know my son's name?" the mother asked.

"Ow, 'e's your son, is 'e?" the flower girl replied. "Well, are you goin' ta pay me for them?" The girl had a very uneducated manner of speaking.

"Do no such thing, Mother," the daughter said.

But the mother paid the flower girl for the ruined flowers, despite her daughter's protests. She even gave the flower girl a few extra pennies.

"Thank you kindly, lady," the flower girl said with a smile.

"Now tell me how you know my son's name," the mother said.

"I don't," the flower girl replied. "I call every stranger Freddy or Charlie when I'm tryin' to be pleasant. Every man in England is named Freddy or Charlie, or somethin' of the sort."

At that moment, an older gentleman rushed into the doorway. He was also soaked, but he was quite distinguished looking. He put his foot up on the pillar base next to the flower girl to fix his trousers. The flower girl saw this as a perfect opportunity to make some money.

"The rain'll soon be done," the flower girl said. "Cheer up, Cap'n. Buy a flower off a poor gal."

"I haven't any small change," the gentleman replied.

"I can give you change," the flower girl insisted.

"I have only large bills," the gentleman said.

"Please," the flower girl begged.

"Here's a penny for you," the gentleman offered. "Now be a good girl and don't be troublesome."

The flower girl was disappointed. She hung her head, but thanked the man, anyway.

A bystander who had observed the

Pygmalion

whole scene walked up to the flower girl.

"Be very careful," he said. "Don't accept the money without giving something in return," he said. "Give the gentleman a flower for that penny. There is a suspicious fellow over there writing down every single word you're saying."

The flower girl turned her head. She was alarmed to see that the bystander was right. A man behind a pillar was carefully recording every word that she had said.

"What's he want, do you think?" she asked the bystander.

"I don't know, but mind what you say," he cautioned.

The flower girl shivered. She was wet and tired. She did not want this strange man writing down things about her. What could he possibly want with her? she wondered.

CHAPTER 2

Professor Henry Higgins

The flower girl was terrified and sprang to her feet at once. "I ain't done nothin' wrong," she said hysterically. "I was only speakin' to the man. I got a right to sell flowers."

The crowd tried to calm the flower girl. They assured her that no one was going to hurt her. They would protect her. The distraught flower girl broke through the mob surrounding her. She ran up to the older gentleman who had given her the money.

"Please don't let 'em arrest me," she begged. "You dunno what it'll do to me!" Her eyes filled with tears.

The man who had been taking notes stepped forward. The rest of the crowd followed closely behind him. "There, there, there," he said. "No one is going to hurt you, you silly girl. What do you take me for?"

"She thought you were a police officer," the bystander said. "He's a gentleman. Just take a look at his boots," he added, turning to the flower girl.

"I swear I didn't do nothin' wrong!" the flower girl screamed.

"Oh, hush up," the notetaker said. "Do I look like a policeman to you?" He was very rude, but meant no harm to the girl.

But the flower girl could not be reassured. She continued to scream and point at the notetaker. "Then what was you writin' down my words for?" she asked. "How do I know you're not writin' lies? You just give me that notepad and show me what it was you were writin'!"

The notetaker opened up his pad and shoved it under the girl's nose so she could read his notes. She looked puzzled. She couldn't read them because the man had written down all of her words phonetically—written as they sound, not as they are spelled.

"I can't read it," said the flower girl. "It ain't proper writin'!"

The notetaker read it for her. He had written down everything she had said to the older gentleman. He reproduced her

pronunciation exactly.

"Is it because I called him Cap'n?" the flower girl asked. "I didn't mean no 'arm. Please sir, don't let him arrest me for usin' a word like that."

"Please, sir," the older gentleman said. "Anyone could plainly see that the girl meant no harm. I appreciate it, but I don't need your protection."

Meanwhile, the crowd was starting to protest against the notetaker. They thought that he was a spy.

"He's not a cop," one bystander said.

"Mind your own business," someone else shouted angrily.

"Leave the poor girl alone," another called. "He's a bloomin' busybody!"

"And how is your family down in Selsey?" the notetaker asked the bystander.

"How do you know that I'm from Selsey?" the bystander asked.

"I just know," the notetaker replied. "I can tell by the way you speak." Then he said to the flower girl, "How is it that you have come so far east? You were born in Lisson Grove."

"It ain't a crime to leave Lisson Grove," the flower girl said. "It ain't good enough for a pig to live in. Boo, hoo, hoo!" She burst into tears.

"You can live wherever you want to live," the notetaker said. "But please stop that awful noise."

"I'm a good girl, I am," the flower girl protested.

"Do you know where I come from?"

another bystander asked.

"Hoxton," replied the notetaker, without hesitation.

The bystander was amazed. "Well, you must know everything," he said.

The flower girl was still quite injured. "'E ain't got no reason to meddle with me, 'e ain't," she cried.

One of the men in the crowd agreed with her. "Of course he hasn't," he said. "Where's your warrant, sir?"

But the rest of the crowd was amazed by the notetaker's ability to pinpoint where they had come from merely by listening to the sounds of their voices.

"Have you ever thought of doing that at the music hall?" the older gentleman asked. "It's quite entertaining."

"The thought has crossed my mind," answered the notetaker, sarcastically.

The flower girl resented the attention that the notetaker was suddenly getting. " 'E's no gentleman, 'e ain't," she cried.

By that time, the rain had stopped

and the crowd was starting to thin out. The mother and daughter were still waiting for Freddy to return with a cab.

"What on earth is Freddy doing?" the daughter cried. She had completely run out of patience.

Without even realizing it, the notetaker had blurted out, "Earls Court. And your mother is from Epsom, no doubt."

"Please keep your remarks to yourself," the daughter snapped.

"I'm sorry," said the notetaker. He had not realized that he said it aloud.

"How interesting," the mother said. "I was brought up very near Epsom!"

The notetaker was very amused by his own accuracy.

"Come along, Clara," the mother said. "I guess we shall be forced to take the bus." She walked off, and Clara angrily stomped off after her.

By that time, everyone, except for the notetaker, the older gentleman, and the flower girl was gone. The flower girl

was trying to rearrange flowers in her basket. Tears streamed down her face.

"'E's no right to take away my character," she muttered. "My character's just as good as any lady's!"

The notetaker started to say something, but the older gentleman made a gesture to be quiet. Together, they watched the flower girl compose herself.

CHAPTER 3
A New Friendship

"May I ask you how you are able to do what you do?" the older gentleman asked the notetaker.

"It's simple phonetics," the notetaker replied. "The science of speech. It's my profession and my hobby. I can place a man's pronunciation within five miles of his hometown."

"'E ought to be ashamed of 'imself," mumbled the flower girl. "Coward!"

"But do you make a good living?" the gentleman asked the notetaker.

"Yes, I make quite a good living," the notetaker replied.

"Let 'im mind 'is own business and leave a poor girl alone," she said.

At her last remark, the notetaker exploded. "Woman, stop your endless boo-hooing this instant," he demanded. "Or leave here immediately."

"I've a right to be 'ere same as you," she shot back angrily.

"A woman who utters such nonsense as you has no right to be anywhere," he said. "Keep in mind that your native tongue is the language of Shakespeare. Don't sit around and babble like an uneducated pigeon!"

The flower girl was stunned by his remarks. Enraged, all she could manage was a cry of rage. "Ah-ah-ah-ow-ow-oo!" she screeched.

"My, my—what a sound," the notetaker commented casually. He was writing down every syllable of the sound. He turned to the gentleman and asked, "Do you see this creature with such awful speech that it will

keep her in the gutter as long as she lives? I could teach her to speak properly. I could even pass her off as a duchess at an ambassador's garden party if I wanted to," he boasted.

"I study dialects myself," the gentleman said. "Mainly Indian dialects."

"You do?" the notetaker said. "You don't happen to know the famous author, Colonel Pickering, do you?"

"I am Colonel Pickering," the gentleman replied. "Who are you?"

"Henry Higgins," the notetaker said, holding out his hand. "Author of *Higgins's Universal Alphabet.*"

"What a lucky coincidence," Pickering said, excitedly shaking his hand. "I just read your book. I was so fascinated by it that I came back from India to meet you! Where do you live?"

"I'm at 27A Wimpole Street. Come and see me tomorrow," Higgins said.

"Why don't we have supper together right now?" Pickering asked.

"Certainly," Higgins replied.

"Buy a flower, kind sir," the flower girl said to Pickering as he passed her. "I don't 'ave enough money for my lodgings."

"Sorry, I haven't any change," Pickering said as he walked away.

"Liar," Higgins said to the flower girl. "Earlier you said that you had enough money to make change. If that's the case, then you should have money for your lodgings."

"You ought to be stuffed with nails," the flower girl said, flinging her basket

at his feet. Before walking away, Higgins grunted and threw a handful of change into her basket.

The flower girl was enraged. "Ah-ow-ooh!" she screamed as she picked up the coins.

Just then, Freddy pulled up in a cab. "I got one," he yelled. "Where are my mother and sister?"

"They took the bus," the flower girl replied, eyeing the cab.

"They left me with a cab on my hands and no use for it!" he said.

"I'll make use of it," the flower girl said as she hopped into the cab. The driver tried to force her out, but as soon as she showed him that she had money, he changed his mind. "Take me to Drury Lane," she ordered.

"I've been had!" Freddy cried.

The cab driver left the flower girl on Drury Lane. It was in the poorer section of town, and was very dismal and dirty. She trudged up the lane, with

her basket in hand, to an alley. At the end of the alley was the building where the flower girl rented a room.

It was a small, dreary room. The wallpaper was hanging off the wall in many places, due to the leaks in the ceiling. One of the windows was broken and taped up. A birdcage stood in the corner, but it was empty. The bird had died long ago, but the girl kept the cage as a reminder.

The room was damp, shabby and

quite bare. The bed was old and falling apart, and the blankets were very worn. The only way to light the room was with a gas lamp, for which the girl had to insert a penny every hour.

The flower girl was quite tired, but she was much too excited to go to bed. She counted all of the money that Higgins had thrown at her. She sat down on the bed and planned what to do with her new riches until the light in the gas lamp went out. Then she took off her shoes, but left all of her clothes on for warmth, and finally went to bed and dreamed about her good fortune.

Colonel Pickering went to Professor Higgins's home early the next morning. Higgins eagerly played his recordings for the colonel. They sat in Higgins's laboratory, which was on the first floor of Higgins's home.

The large room was filled with interesting things. Two tall file cabinets stood against opposite walls. A flat writing table stood in the corner. On the table were a phonograph machine and a laryngoscope, which Higgins used to examine the larynx. Higgins also had a sculpture of a human head that he

used when he did his research.

Further into the room was a big fireplace with a comfortable sofa in front of it. Higgins also had a grand piano.

Pickering sat at the table, and Higgins stood very close to him. Higgins was a very scientific sort of man. But he was quite childlike in his excitement to show Pickering all of his findings.

"Well, I believe that I have played all of my recordings for you," Higgins said to Pickering.

"Quite fascinating," Pickering answered, gazing in awe at the man.

"Would you like to hear them again?" Higgins asked.

"No, thank you," Pickering said as he moved to the sofa in front of the fireplace. "I was rather proud of myself for pronouncing twenty-four distinct vowel sounds. But your hundred and thirty-three beat me! I can barely hear the difference between them."

Higgins chuckled. He took some sweets from a plate on top of the piano. "You'll be able to hear the difference with some practice," he said.

Mrs. Pearce, Higgins's housekeeper, looked into the room. She hesitated before announcing, "There is a young woman here to see you, sir."

"Well, what does she want?" Higgins demanded in his gruff manner.

"Sir, she says that you'll be glad to see her," Mrs. Pearce answered. "She's a very common girl. I would have turned her away, only I figured that

you might like to have her talk into your machines. I hope I have not done anything wrong, sir, but you do sometimes have strange people in your lab."

"It's all right," Higgins said. "Does she have an unusual accent?"

"It's dreadful, sir," Mrs. Pearce replied, shuddering at the thought of the girl's voice.

"This might be interesting," Higgins said excitedly to Pickering. "Show her up, Mrs. Pearce." The housekeeper went at once to get the young woman.

"What a stroke of luck," Higgins said. "Pickering, now I will be able to show you how I work."

Mrs. Pearce returned with the flower girl following closely behind her. The girl wore a hat with orange, red, and blue feathers in it. She had an almost-clean apron on, and a worn coat that she had made as neat as possible for her visit.

Higgins was disappointed. "This is the girl I studied last night," he said. "I already have all the information I need about Lisson Grove." Turning toward the girl, he said, "Please leave. I have no use for you."

"Don't be so quick," the flower girl replied.

"Mind your manners, girl," Mrs. Pearce said. "Do you think a gentleman like Professor Higgins has time for you?" She pulled the girl toward the door.

"You ain't 'eard what I come for," said the flower girl. "Did you tell 'im I come in a taxi?"

"Why should Professor Higgins care how you arrived?" Mrs. Pearce asked.

"'E ain't above givin' lessons, is 'e?" the flower girl asked. "I 'eard 'im say 'e gave lessons. I come to 'ave lessons, I 'ave, and pay for 'em, too, make no mistake. But if my money ain't good enough, I'll leave!"

"How, exactly, do you expect me to respond to this request?" Higgins asked.

"Ain't you gonna offer me a seat?" the flower girl asked. "A real gentleman would," she challenged him.

Higgins turned to Pickering and said, "Shall we ask this creature to sit or should we throw her out?" he asked.

"Ah-ah-ow-ow-oo!" the flower girl screamed again. "I won't be called a creature when I've offered to pay like a proper lady!"

She ran toward the piano, terrified that Higgins was serious about throwing her out. Higgins and Pickering stared at her from across the room.

"What exactly do you want, my girl?" Pickering asked gently.

"I want to work in a flower shop instead of selling flowers on street corners," the flower girl replied. "But they won't let me unless I can talk more proper. 'E said 'e'd 'elp me. I'm 'ere to pay. I ain't asking for no favors!"

"What a foolish girl," said Mrs. Pearce. "What makes you think you

can afford lessons?"

"I know what lessons cost, I do," the flower girl insisted.

"How much do you think lessons cost?" Higgins asked, giving her a chance.

"I knew you'd come around once you saw the chance to get back some of the money you threw at me last night," the flower girl said.

"Sit down," Higgins demanded.

"Do as you're told," Mrs. Pearce said. She placed an empty chair between Higgins and Pickering.

"Ah-ah-ow-ow-oo!" the flower girl screamed. She did not like taking orders.

"Please sit down." Pickering said courteously.

The flower girl said, "Don't mind if I do." She sat down in the empty chair.

"What's your name?" Higgins asked the flower girl.

"Eliza Doolittle," she replied.

"How much do you plan to pay me

for the lessons?" Higgins asked.

"My friend pays eighteen pence an hour for French lessons from a real Frenchman," Eliza said. "I'll pay you a shilling. You can't expect me to pay you more than that for teaching me my own language. Take it or leave it."

"If you think of a shilling as a percentage of this girl's income, it's the same as sixty pounds from a millionaire," Higgins said to Pickering. He paced back and forth, shaking the keys and money around in his pocket, suddenly excited about the idea.

"How so?" Pickering asked.

"She's offering me two-fifths of her day's income," Higgins explained. "Two-fifths of a millionaire's income for a day is about sixty pounds. By George, it's the best offer I've ever had!"

Eliza got up out of the chair. She was nervous. "Sixty pounds!" she cried. "I didn't offer sixty pounds. I ain't got—"

"Hold your tongue," Higgins ordered. "If you don't stop that silly whining, I'll take a broomstick to you."

"Just like me father," Eliza said. "Ah-ah-ow-ow-oo!" she screeched. She wiped her nose on her sleeve.

"If I decide to teach you," Higgins said, "I'll be worse than two fathers."

He took the handkerchief out of his pocket and offered it to Eliza.

"What's this for?" Eliza asked.

"To wipe your eyes," Higgins said.

"Always use this and not your sleeve if you wish to be a lady."

Eliza just stared at him helplessly. She was confused. Mrs. Pearce tried to explain to Higgins that Eliza didn't understand such things. She took the handkerchief away from Eliza. But Eliza quickly snatched it back.

"Give that back," Eliza said. "'E give it to me, not you!"

Pickering laughed at the scene. Then he turned to Higgins and said, "I'll make a bet with you. I'll pay for the lessons if you can turn the girl into a lady in time for the ambassador's garden party in six months."

"You're real good," Eliza said to Pickering. "Thank you, sir." She wasn't used to being treated so nicely.

Higgins was tempted by the offer. He loved a challenge. "It's irresistible," he said. "She's so low and dirty."

"I washed my face before I come, I did," Eliza protested.

Higgins grew more excited as the idea of the bet grew on him. "A chance like this doesn't come along every day," he said. "I'll make a duchess of this ragged guttersnipe!"

"Ah-ah-ow-ow-oo!" Eliza yelled. She was angry at Higgins for talking about her in such a way.

"In six months, I'll be able to pass her off as a lady," Higgins said. "We'll start immediately. Mrs. Pearce, give her a bath and scrub her clean. Then burn her clothes. Wrap her in brown paper until we get her some new clothes. Wallop her if she gives you trouble."

Eliza jumped up and took shelter between Pickering and Mrs. Pearce.

"Be reasonable, sir," Mrs. Pearce said. "You really can't walk all over her like this."

"I'm going to leave," Eliza said.

"Fine," Higgins replied. "Throw her out, Mrs. Pearce. Don't order the new clothes."

Eliza was very close to bursting into tears. She stormed across the room and threw the handkerchief at Higgins. He picked up the handkerchief and blocked Eliza from leaving the room.

"You're an ungrateful, wicked girl," Higgins said to Eliza. "This is the thanks I get for trying to pull you out of the gutter and make a lady of you."

"Sir, I won't allow this experiment," Mrs. Pearce said. "Where are your parents, girl?"

Eliza drew closer to Mrs. Pearce and said that her mother had died when

she was young. Her sixth stepmother threw her out a few years earlier. The stepmother thought that Eliza was old enough to earn her own living.

"See, she is of no use to anyone but me," said Higgins.

"But what is to become of her when the experiment is over?" asked Mrs. Pearce. "Will you pay her?"

"She'll have food and clothes," Higgins replied. "She'll only get into trouble if she has too much money."

"Does it occur to you that she has feelings?" Pickering asked Higgins.

"Sir, what is to become of her when you're done?" Mrs. Pearce asked again.

"That's not my concern," Higgins replied curtly.

"You've no feelings, you brute," Eliza screamed. Her fists were clenched in rage at Higgins's insults.

She started to make her way toward the door again. This time Higgins lured her back with a plate of chocolates that

sat on the piano.

"'Ow do I know they ain't poisoned?" Eliza asked.

Higgins took out a knife and cut the chocolate in half. He ate one of the pieces to show Eliza that it was safe. When Eliza opened her mouth to say something, Higgins quickly popped the other piece into her mouth. Eliza ate the chocolate.

"If you stay, you can have boxes of chocolate every day," offered Higgins. "Think of it Eliza—chocolate, taxis, diamonds!"

"It's not fair to tempt her," Mrs. Pearce said, feeling sorry for the girl.

"I'm a good girl, I am," Eliza said, trying to be dignified.

"And so you shall remain," Higgins said. "And one day you will marry a handsome officer. He will be swept away by your beauty."

"Higgins, if this girl is to take part in this experiment," said Pickering, "she must understand exactly what is to happen."

"Ah-ah-ow-oo!" Eliza yelled.

"That's all you'll get from Eliza," Higgins replied. "Yelling and shouting. There's no use in explaining things to her. Eliza, you will live here for the next six months and learn how to speak beautifully. If you are good, you'll sleep in a nice bedroom. If you're bad, you'll sleep in the kitchen and Mrs. Pearce will wallop you. At the end of six months, you will go to Buckingham Palace. If you pass for a duchess, you will get a sum of money to start a new life. If you don't pass, you will be taken away by the police. Can I be any clearer?"

"Oh, I'll explain it to her in private," Mrs. Pearce said. "I know you don't mean any harm, Mr. Higgins, but when you get interested in your work like this, you just don't think of what can happen to people."

"Very well," Higgins said. "Take her off to the bathroom."

"You're a bully, you are," Eliza

screamed. "I won't be walloped and I won't stay here if I don't want to!"

Mrs. Pearce led Eliza out of the room. Even after they were gone, Eliza's screams and complaints could still be heard.

After a few moments, Mrs. Pearce came back into the room, carrying Eliza's dirty clothes. "Sir, may I have a word with you?" Mrs. Pearce asked Higgins.

"Certainly," Higgins said.

"Please be very careful of the way you speak around Eliza," Mrs. Pearce requested.

"I'm always careful," Higgins said.

"You have a very bad habit of swearing when things don't go your way," Mrs. Pearce said. "I don't want the girl to pick up that habit."

Pickering laughed and nodded in agreement.

"Very well," Higgins said.

"Also sir, please do not come down

to breakfast in your robe," said Mrs. Pearce. "It's not appropriate attire with a guest in the house. And please do not wipe you fingers on your sleeves, as you usually do."

"I only do those things if I am forgetful," Higgins yelled angrily. "I don't make a habit of it. But, very well, Mrs. Pearce, I will be careful around the girl," Higgins huffed.

With a doubtful grin on her face, Mrs. Pearce left the room to tend to Eliza.

"Honestly," Higgins said, "I don't

know where that woman ever got the idea that I was cross and overbearing."

Pickering nodded sympathetically. To himself he chucked, "I really can't imagine!"

CHAPTER 5

Eliza Cleans Up

Eliza thought that Mrs. Pearce was going to take her down into the basement. But, much to her surprise, Eliza was led up to the third floor instead. Once upstairs, Mrs. Pearce showed Eliza to the spare bedroom.

"This will be your bedroom," Mrs. Pearce said.

"I can't stay 'ere," Eliza said. "It's much too good for the likes of me. I'd be afraid to touch anything. I ain't a duchess yet, you know."

"Once you make yourself as clean as the room, you won't be afraid of it," Mrs.

Pearce reassured her. She opened a door, revealing a large, modern bathroom.

"Blimey, what's that?" Eliza asked.

"It's a bathroom. It is where I am going to wash you," Mrs. Pearce replied. Eliza was alarmed. She did not like the idea of getting her entire body wet. She had never had a proper bath in her whole life.

She told Mrs. Pearce that she knew a woman who had died from bathing. Mrs. Pearce explained that Eliza would have to be clean and smell nice if she was to study with Higgins and Pickering.

"Professor Higgins takes an ice-cold bath every day," she said.

"That man's made of iron, 'e is," said Eliza, shaking her head.

"There are two taps—hot and cold," Mrs. Pearce said. "You can make the water any temperature you like."

Eliza burst into tears.

"Stop crying," Mrs. Pearce scolded.

"Go and undress."

"I can't. I won't," Eliza said. "It ain't decent. I've never taken off all of me clothes in me life!"

"Do you mean that you sleep in the clothes that you wear during the day?" asked an amazed Mrs. Pearce.

"What else do I have to sleep in?" Eliza replied.

"You'll never have to do that as long as you live here," said Mrs. Pearce. "I will get you a proper nightgown."

Finally, Mrs. Pearce managed to get the girl out of her clothes and into the bathtub. She put on a pair of rubber gloves, sprinkled bubble bath into the water, and began to scrub Eliza with a long-handle brush, causing Eliza to scream.

Eventually, Eliza noticed the soft feeling of the bubbles and the nice scent. The warm water felt good. She did not have running water in Drury Lane. She knew a few people who had

running water, but it was cold and rusty.

Although she was still angry at Higgins's rude behavior, she was touched by Colonel Pickering's kindness. And Mrs. Pearce had not walloped her yet. Eliza began to relax a little. She even started to think about her new clothes.

Meanwhile, Mrs. Pearce scrubbed away at the layers of dirt that had become a second skin on Eliza. She tried to behave, but Eliza couldn't help letting out a few angry shouts. Life with Henry Higgins was going to take some getting used to, she thought.

A short while later, Mrs. Pearce returned to Higgins's lab. She was quite distressed. She said that there was a man at the door. His name was Alfred Doolittle, and he claimed that Eliza was his daughter.

"Send him up," Higgins said.

"I hope he doesn't give us any trou-

ble," Pickering said.

"Don't worry," Higgins said. "He'll get more trouble out of me."

Mrs. Pearce showed Doolittle into the room. He was an older man, but appeared quite lively. He wore a dustman's hat with a brim that came down to his neck and shoulders.

"I come about a serious matter," Doolittle said.

"What do you want?" Higgins asked.

"I want me daughter," Doolittle demanded.

"Fine, take her," Higgins said. "You're her father. You don't think that I am going to take care of your daughter for you, do you?"

Doolittle was startled. "Is this fair?" he asked. "You have me daughter. What do I get out of it?"

"Your daughter had the nerve to come here and ask for speech lessons," Higgins said. "I think you sent her here so you could blackmail me."

"No, I didn't," Doolittle said.

"Then how did you know she was here?" Higgins asked. "I'll report you to the police for bribery."

"I swear I ain't seen the girl in two months," Doolittle said nervously, looking down.

He explained to Higgins and Pickering that the man who had driven Eliza's taxi that morning was her landlady's son. Eliza had sent the man back for her luggage. He had run into Doolittle on the way and told him where he had dropped Eliza off that morning. "What was I to think?" Doolittle asked.

"So you came to rescue her," Higgins said. "Well, take her away then!"

"I didn't say nothin' about taking 'er back, did I?" said Doolittle.

Higgins called out to Mrs. Pearce to deliver Eliza to her father. Mrs. Pearce quickly entered the room and reminded Higgins that it would be impossible, since he had ordered her to burn Eliza's old clothes and the new ones had not yet been delivered.

Doolittle seemed very troubled at the thought of taking his daughter back.

"Listen 'ere," Doolittle said in a hushed tone to Higgins. "Me and you is men of the world, ain't we?"

"Oh, we are, are we?" Higgins said.

"I'm willing to make an arrangement," Doolittle said. "If you want the girl, you can have her. She ain't worth much to me as a daughter. She's worth more as a woman. I'll take five pounds for 'er."

"Higgins's intentions are very honorable," Pickering interrupted.

"You callous rascal," Higgins said. "You would sell your own daughter for five pounds?"

"To oblige a gentleman like you, I would," Doolittle said.

"Have you no morals?" Pickering asked, with a look of disgust.

"Can't afford 'em," Doolittle replied. "I ain't pretending to be deserving of anything."

"Well, I suppose we should pay the man," Higgins said.

"He'll make bad use of the money," Pickering said.

"I won't," Doolittle said. "It'll be gone by Monday, knowing me and me girlfriend. Then I'll go to work, same as if I never 'ad it."

Higgins paid Doolittle. Pickering asked why Doolittle didn't marry his girlfriend. He explained that he wanted to, but that she was unwilling. It made Doolittle angry, he said, because he didn't have the same rights that he

would if he were her husband.

"Marry Eliza while she is still young," Doolittle instructed Higgins. "If you don't, *you'll* be sorry, but if you do, *she'll* be sorry. But better 'er than you; she's just a woman."

Higgins could stand no more of the conversation. "Take the money and be on your way," he shouted.

"Thank you, sir," Doolittle said as he turned to leave. He hurried toward the door. As he swung the door open, he came face to face with a beautiful, dainty girl being led into the room by Mrs. Pearce.

Eliza was dressed in an exquisite blue kimono decorated with white flowers. Doolittle apologized to her for being in her way, and proceeded to leave.

"Don't you know your own daughter?" the girl asked. She moved closer to Doolittle, so he could get a better look.

"It's Eliza!" exclaimed Doolittle. "I

never thought she'd clean up as good as this!"

Higgins and Pickering were also shocked by the sight of a clean, well-dressed Eliza.

"It's easy to clean up 'ere," said Eliza. "'Ot and cold water, as much as you like, there is. Soft towels and brushes, there is. Now I know why proper ladies is so clean!"

"I'm glad the bathroom met your approval," Higgins said.

Eliza told him that there was one thing about the bathroom that she disliked: the mirror. She was not used to

seeing herself without clothes on. She told him that she had hung a towel over it.

"You've brought your daughter up quite strictly," Higgins said to Doolittle.

"I ain't brought 'er up at all," Doolittle said, "except to 'it her with the strap now and again. Don't worry, she'll pick up your ways easy."

"I'll pick up nothing," said Eliza. "I'm a good girl, I am."

"If you say again that you're a good girl, your father shall take you home," said Higgins.

"No, 'e won't," Eliza said. "All 'e come 'ere for was money." She turned and stuck out her tongue at her father. Doolittle became so enraged that he reached to grab her. Pickering had to come between them to stop the fight. Higgins suggested that Doolittle leave, unless he had some last words of father-ly advice for Eliza. He said he didn't, but he instructed Higgins to take his strap to Eliza if she didn't listen.

"Come visit the girl often," Higgins said.

"I have a job quite far off right now," Doolittle said. "But maybe later." With that, he was gone.

"You won't see 'im in a 'urry," Eliza said. "'E's a liar, and I don't care to see 'im ever again."

"What does he do for a living, Eliza?" Pickering asked.

"Swindles people out of money," Eliza replied. "Please call me Miss Doolittle. It sounds so genteel."

Eliza asked Higgins if she could take

a taxi to her old neighborhood. She said she wanted to show her new appearance to the people she lived near and make them jealous. Pickering suggested that she wait until she received her new fashionable clothes.

"Besides, you don't want to be a snob," Higgins said.

Mrs. Pearce came back into the room and announced that Eliza's new clothes had arrived. Eliza squealed with delight and rushed out of the room.

"Don't rush about like that, girl," Mrs. Pearce said. She followed Eliza out of the room to see her new wardrobe.

"We have taken on quite a job," Higgins declared.

"We certainly have, Higgins!" Pickering agreed.

CHAPTER 6
Eliza's First Lesson

Eliza's first lesson began early the next morning. She was dressed in her fancy new clothes, and was quite full from the hearty breakfast that she had been served. She was not used to having enough food. She took her seat in the lab, between Colonel Pickering and Professor Higgins.

Higgins, by nature, was not able to sit still. He kept rising from his chair and walking around the room. His behavior made Eliza nervous—more nervous than she was to begin with. But Pickering's calm and comforting presence reassured Eliza. If it weren't

for him, she might have run away and never come back!

"Say your alphabet," Higgins ordered, to begin the lesson.

"I know me alphabet," Eliza said. "Do you think I know nothing? I don't need to be taught like a child."

"Say your alphabet!" Higgins repeated, this time more loudly.

"Do say the alphabet, please," Pickering said gently. "You will soon understand the reason for it. Let Professor Higgins teach you in his own way."

"All right, if you put it like that," Eliza said. "Ai-ee, Bi-ee, Cee—"

"Stop, stop, stop!" Higgins yelled. "Listen to this, Pickering. This is the education that our taxes pay for. This poor animal has been locked up in school for years, at our expense, to learn proper English, and this is what she sounds like! Now, say 'A, B, C.'"

"But I am sayin' it," cried Eliza. With that, she repeated the same awful-sounding alphabet as before.

"Stop!" Higgins yelled. "Repeat after me. Say 'a cup of tea'."

"A cappa ti-ee," Eliza said.

"Put your tongue forward until it pushes against the top of your lower teeth," Higgins demanded. Eliza frowned. "Now say 'cup,'" Higgins said.

"C-c-c—I can't," Eliza cried. "I can't say cup."

"Very good," Pickering said. "Splendid, Miss Doolittle." Eliza was very encouraged by Pickering's praise.

"By George, she's done it on the first try," Higgins said. "Pickering, we shall make a duchess of her yet. Now Eliza, do you think you can say 'tea' properly? If you say it as you did before, you shall be dragged around by the hair on your head."

Eliza was in tears. Although Higgins didn't really mean what he had said, Eliza didn't know that.

"I don't hear no difference between the way you say it and the way I do. Except when you say it, it sounds more

genteel-like," she sobbed.

"Well, if you can hear that difference, why on earth are you crying?" asked Higgins.

"It's all right, Eliza," Pickering comforted. "It's all right if you cry a little bit. The lessons won't hurt. I promise you that. I promise that I won't let him drag you around by your hair."

"Go find Mrs. Pearce," Higgins said to Eliza. "Practice it on your own. We'll have another lesson at half-past four this afternoon. Off with you!"

Eliza rushed out of the room, still sobbing. She knew that she was going to have to endure these humiliating lessons for months before she would be able to go out in public.

CHAPTER 7
The First Test

After two months of long, difficult speech lessons with Eliza, Higgins decided that it was time to test his experiment on a small audience. Today was his mother's day for entertaining visitors at her apartment, and Higgins thought that this was his perfect opportunity. The company had not yet arrived when Higgins showed up.

Mrs. Higgins's home was lovely. It was not crowded, like her son's home. There was a door in one wall that opened onto a small balcony. The balcony had a view of the river. Against the adjacent wall was a big fireplace.

The sitting room contained beautiful antique furniture. There were a few tasteful oil paintings hanging on the walls and a small piano. Plenty of comfortable chairs seemed to invite guests to sit. The room was warm and peaceful.

It was late in the afternoon when Higgins arrived at his mother's home. Mrs. Higgins was waiting for her guests when Higgins burst roughly into the room with his hat on. He bent down to kiss his mother.

"Oh, Henry," Mrs. Higgins said. "What are you doing here? You know that today I receive visitors. You promised me that you wouldn't come."

"I know what I promised," Higgins said, throwing his hat upon the table. "I came on purpose."

"Go home at once," Mrs. Higgins ordered. "You offend all of my friends and they stop coming around after they meet you."

"Nonsense," Higgins replied, ignoring her orders and taking a seat on the sofa. "I'm not good at small talk, but people don't mind."

"Oh, really," Mrs. Higgins said raising her eyebrows. "Never mind your small talk. It's your large talk that worries me!"

"I must stay," Higgins said. "I have a job for you. It involves phonetics."

"Sorry. I can't help you," Mrs. Higgins said. "I'm afraid that I don't understand your vowel studies. I enjoy receiving the postcards written in your shorthand, but I enjoy reading the copies written in plain English that you send along with them even more."

Higgins explained to his mother that the job did not involve her understanding of phonetics, but someone else's. He told her that he had met a girl. Mrs. Higgins was excited at the thought of her son falling in love with a girl he had met, but she was very disappointed

when Higgins explained that that wasn't the case.

"What a pity," Mrs. Higgins said.

"I can't be bothered with young women," Higgins said. "My idea of the perfect woman is someone who is as much like you as possible, and she doesn't exist. All young women are idiots." He abruptly got up from his seat and started pacing the room, jingling his keys in his pocket.

"Tell me about the girl, Henry," Mrs. Higgins said.

"She's a common flower girl I found on the street," Higgins said bluntly.

"And you invited her to my home?" asked a shocked Mrs. Higgins.

"Don't worry," said Higgins. "I've taught her to speak properly. Her manners aren't perfect yet, but I've ordered her to be on her best behavior. She's only to speak of two safe subjects: the weather, and everyone's health."

"How can you be so silly, Henry?"

Mrs. Higgins asked.

Higgins assured his mother that all would turn out well. He mentioned Pickering's involvement to reassure her.

Mrs. Higgins looked doubtful, even angry, with her son.

Ignoring her obvious concern, Higgins told his mother about the bet that he and Pickering had made and about trying to pass Eliza off as a duchess in six months. Eliza was a great student, he said—she caught on very quickly. She had the pronunciation right, but her topics of conversation still needed work.

Mrs. Higgins listened to her son, astonished. She merely looked at him and shook her head, while he continued to look quite pleased with himself. He was sure he would win his bet.

CHAPTER 8
❋
The Guests Arrive

Just then, the parlor maid entered to announce the guests' arrival. "Mrs. and Miss Eynsford Hill," she said.

Mrs. and Miss Eynsford Hill came in. They were the mother and daughter who had been waiting for Freddy to hail them a cab in the rain the night that Higgins first met Eliza. The mother was very wellbred and quiet. The daughter seemed to be comfortable in social circles.

Although they were not rich, they were quite genteel. They politely shook hands with Mrs. Higgins. Higgins tried to snatch his hat from the table and escape, but his mother caught his arm before he had the chance.

"This is my son, Henry," Mrs. Higgins said, introducing him to the guests.

"Your celebrated son," Mrs. Hill said. "I have been waiting to meet you!"

"Delighted," Higgins said glumly. Instead of moving toward her, he backed against the piano and bowed. "I believe I've seen you both before, but I can't remember where. It doesn't matter. You'd better sit down," he said rudely.

"I'm sorry to say that my celebrated son hasn't any manners," apologized Mrs. Higgins. "Don't mind him."

"I don't mind him at all," Miss Hill said gaily as she took a seat.

"I didn't mean to be rude," Higgins said. He stood at the window, with his back to the company.

The parlor maid returned to the room, with Pickering following. "Colonel Pickering," the maid announced.

"How do you do, Mrs. Higgins?" Pickering asked politely.

"So glad you've come," Mrs. Higgins replied. She introduced Pickering to Mrs. Hill and her daughter. Pickering pulled up a chair and sat between Mrs. Higgins and Mrs. Hill.

"Has Henry told you the reason for our visit today?" Pickering asked.

"We were abruptly interrupted!" Higgins said angrily over his shoulder.

"Henry, really!" cried an embarrassed Mrs. Higgins.

"Are we in the way?" Mrs. Hill asked. She had half-risen out of her chair, when Mrs. Higgins came over and asked her to please stay.

"You couldn't have come at a better time," Mrs. Higgins assured her. "We want you to meet a friend of ours."

This caught Higgins's attention. He was excited again when he was reminded of showing off Eliza's new speaking skills.

"By George," he said, "we need two or three people. You'll do as well as anyone else."

Once again the parlor maid stepped into the room, this time with a young man following her. "Mr. Eynsford Hill," the parlor maid said. It was Freddy, the man who had been trying to hail a taxi for his mother and sister in the rain that fateful night in Covent Garden.

"Oh, no! Another of them," Higgins sighed.

Freddy shook hands with his hostess, who introduced him to Colonel Pickering and Higgins.

"I'll take an oath that I've met you somewhere before," Higgins said. He looked Freddy over as though he were a pickpocket. "Where was it?"

"I don't think we've met," Freddy answered.

"It's no matter, anyway," Higgins said. "Sit down." He shook Freddy's hand and practically flung him onto the sofa. "Now, what on earth are we going to talk about until Eliza arrives?"

"You are the life of all of the Royal Society's fancy parties, Henry," said Mrs. Higgins. "But you have absolutely no skills for commonplace functions."

"I sympathize," Miss Hill said. She had been watching Higgins the entire time and considered him to be a very eligible bachelor. "I don't make small talk. If only people would just say what they really think."

"That would never do!" Higgins shouted. Do you think it would be a good idea for me to say what I am really thinking right now?"

"Is it really that bad?" Miss Hill asked coyly.

"I assure you that it's completely rude," replied Higgins.

"I'm sure you don't mean that," Miss Hill replied.

"I most surely do," replied Higgins. "We are all savages at heart. We're supposed to be cultured and civilized, but how many of us really are? Mrs.

Hill, what do you know about science? Miss Hill, what do you know of poetry? Freddy, do you know anything about either topic? What the devil do you imagine I know of philosophy?"

"Or of manners," added Mrs. Higgins. She was trying, as politely as she could in the presence of company, to warn her son to stop his ranting.

Just then, the parlor maid entered one more time. She announced, "Miss Doolittle." The moment had finally come for Higgins to put his student to her first test.

CHAPTER 9

A Grand Entrance

As Eliza entered the room, Higgins hastily ran over to his mother. "Here she is, Mother," Higgins said. He stood on his tiptoes and made signs over his mother's head to indicate to Eliza which of the ladies was the hostess.

Eliza was exquisitely dressed that afternoon. She made such an impression of distinction and beauty that the guests rose to their feet, quite charmed by her. Guided by Higgins's signals, she gracefully made her way over to Mrs. Higgins.

"How do you do, Mrs. Higgins?" Eliza said carefully. She spoke with beautiful

tone and with perfect pronunciation. She was even able to pronounce the "h" sound at the beginning of words! "Mr. Higgins asked me to come," she added.

"Yes, indeed. I am very glad to meet you," Mrs. Higgins said.

"How do you do, Miss Doolittle?" asked Colonel Pickering.

"Colonel Pickering, is it not?" asked Eliza, also keeping up the charade. She shook Pickering's hand.

Mrs. Hill said, "I have the strangest feeling that we have met somewhere before. I think I remember your eyes."

"How do you do?" Eliza asked as she sat down gracefully on an ottoman.

Mrs. Hill introduced Eliza to her daughter, Clara, and her son, Freddy. Clara sat down and stared at Eliza.

"I certainly feel like I've met you before," Freddy said, reaching out his hand. He bowed before he took his seat. His eyes remained fixed on Eliza. He was obviously infatuated with her.

"By George!" Higgins said. The

entire party turned to stare at him. He had just realized where he had seen the Eynsford Hillses—in Covent Garden! He was very worried that they might recognize Eliza as the poor flower girl they had seen that night. He sat on the edge of Mrs. Higgins's writing table.

"Henry, please!" cried Mrs. Higgins. "Don't sit on my table. You'll break it."

"Sorry," said Higgins. As he made his way over to the sofa, he clumsily fell over some fire irons on his way. He muttered to himself. Frustrated, he flung himself upon the sofa, nearly breaking it.

Mrs. Higgins was again quite embarrassed, but she managed to control herself and not scold her son. A long, uncomfortable silence followed.

To break the silence, Mrs. Higgins asked, "Will it rain today, do you think?"

"The shallow depression in the west

of these islands is likely to move in an easterly direction," Eliza replied. "There are no indications of any great change in the barometrical situation." She had worked hard to perfect her speech.

"How awfully funny," Freddy said, laughing.

"What is wrong with that, young man?" Eliza asked. "I bet I got it right!" She had almost forgotten herself and reverted back to her old way of speaking!

"I hope it won't turn cold," added

Mrs. Hill. "There's so much influenza about. Our entire family gets it every spring."

"I had an aunt who died of influenza," said Eliza in a tragic tone. "Or so they said. I believe they done the old woman in."

Mrs. Higgins was puzzled. "What do you mean by 'done in'?" she asked.

"Well," Eliza said, "why should she die of influenza when she survived diphtheria just fine the year before? She was blue with it; I saw her with my own eyes. They thought she was dead."

"Dear me," gasped Mrs. Hill.

"Would a woman of that strength die of influenza?" Eliza asked. "And someone stole her straw hat that was supposed to go to me. It was the same person that done her in, I bet."

"What does 'doing her in' mean?" Mrs. Hill asked.

Higgins hastily tried to avoid an awkward situation and stop Eliza from slipping back into her old speaking patterns. "That's the new stylish small talk," said Higgins. "To 'do a person in' means to kill them."

Mrs. Hill was horrified. "Surely, you don't believe that someone killed your aunt, do you?" she asked Eliza.

"Sure I do!" said Eliza. "Them she lived with would have killed her for a hat pin, let alone a hat!"

As Eliza was talking, she noticed that Freddy was snickering. She asked him what he was laughing at.

"You're awfully good at the new small talk," Freddy said.

"If I was doing it properly, what were you laughing at?" she asked him. Then she turned to Higgins and asked, "Have I said anything I shouldn't have said?"

"Not at all, Miss Doolittle," Mrs. Higgins said.

"That's a relief," Eliza said. "What I always say is—"

Before Eliza could say anything

more that might ruin the experiment, Higgins stood up and looked at his watch. He cleared his throat loudly enough to catch Eliza's attention. Eliza looked at him and got the hint.

"Well, I must go," Eliza said, standing up. Everyone in the room rose to their feet. Freddy went to the door to see Eliza out. "So pleased to have met you," Eliza continued. "Good-bye." She shook Mrs. Higgins's hand.

"Good-bye, Miss Doolittle," Colonel Pickering said as he shook Eliza's hand, giving her a slight smile.

Eliza said her good-byes to the rest of the party.

"Are you going to walk across the park?" Freddy asked Eliza, opening the door for her. "If so—"

"Walk?" Eliza said. "Not blooming likely. I am going to take a taxi." With that, she walked out of the room.

Pickering gasped at Eliza's language. Freddy ran out to the balcony to catch a last glimpse of Eliza before she got in the taxi.

Mrs. Hill was quite in shock. "I must say, I am very old-fashioned," she said. "I just can't get used to the new ways at all."

"Oh, Mother," Clara gasped. "People will think that we never go anywhere or see anybody."

"I can't help it," said Mrs. Hill. "I do hope that you won't begin using the expressions that Miss Doolittle used. I have gotten used to you referring to everything as beastly and filthy, although I do not think it is ladylike. But this is too much. Don't you agree, Colonel Pickering?"

"I'm afraid that I am the wrong person to ask," Pickering replied. "I have been away in India so long, and manners have changed so much."

"It's just a habit," argued Clara. "Nobody means anything by it. It is so quaint and gives everything a smart emphasis. I find the new small talk quite delightful."

"Well, I think it is time for us to go," said Mrs. Hill. "We have three more homes to visit."

Pickering and Higgins rose to see the guests off. Clara said her good-byes.

"Be sure to try out the new small talk on your next visit," Higgins ordered.

"I will," Clara promised, smiling. "This Victorian prudery is such stifling nonsense!"

"Such blooming nonsense!" said Higgins forcefully.

"Such blooming nonsense is right," repeated Clara.

"Clara!" cried Mrs. Hill, ashamed. "You mustn't mind Clara. We are so poor, and she gets to go to so few parties. She doesn't quite know how to behave."

"Freddy, would you like to meet Miss Doolittle again?" Mrs. Higgins asked. She had noticed that, clearly, Freddy was smitten with Eliza.

"Yes, I would," Freddy said, eagerly

jumping at the chance.

"Well, you know my days for visitors," said Mrs. Higgins.

With that, the Eynsford Hillses left Mrs. Higgins's home.

CHAPTER 10

Mrs. Higgins's Reaction

Higgins could hardly wait for the guests to leave. He was very eager to find out his mother's reaction to Eliza.

"Well," Higgins demanded. "Is Eliza presentable or not?"

"You silly boy," Mrs. Higgins replied. "Of course she is not presentable. Yes, she can speak properly, the way you have taught her, and she looks beautiful in the clothes you have bought for her. But she gives her true self away with every sentence she utters."

"But don't you think there is possibility?" Pickering asked. "I mean, something can certainly be done to eliminate the nastiness from her topics of conversation."

"Not as long as she is left in Henry's hands," Mrs. Higgins answered.

"Do you mean to say that my language is improper?" Higgins asked.

"On a canal barge, no," said Mrs. Higgins. "But at a garden party, yes."

Higgins was insulted by the remark.

"Come, Henry," Pickering said. "You must admit that your language is often harsh and inappropriate."

"I suppose I don't always speak like

a bishop," Higgins admitted.

Mrs. Higgins asked Pickering exactly what was going on at her son's apartment on Wimpole Street. Pickering was happy to change the subject. He cheerfully explained that he had gone to live there. It made working together on his Indian dialects much more convenient.

"Yes, yes," said Mrs. Higgins. "That sounds quite lovely. But where does Eliza live?"

"With us, of course," Higgins said. "Where else would she live?"

"But on what terms?" Mrs. Higgins asked. "If she's not a servant, what is she? You must be specific."

"I have had to work with that girl every day for two months to get her to where she is today," Higgins said. "Besides, she is quite useful to have around. She knows where all of my things are and she remembers all of my appointments and such."

"How does your housekeep-

er get along with her?" Mrs. Higgins inquired.

"Mrs. Pearce is jolly glad to have Eliza around," Higgins said. "Before Eliza came, Mrs. Pearce had to find things for me. But she does seem to have some silly ideas. She constantly tells me that I don't think clearly where Eliza is concerned."

"Yes," Pickering agreed, "that's the conclusion of every conversation about Eliza."

Higgins argued that he did nothing but think of Eliza, her vowels and consonants and her speech. He was worn out from thinking about her.

"You certainly do like to play with your living doll," Mrs. Higgins observed.

"I'm hardly playing, Mother," Higgins said. "This is one of the hardest jobs I've ever had. It is extremely interesting to take a human being and change her into a whole new person by creating new speech for her."

Pickering pulled his chair closer to

Mrs. Higgins. He bent over her as he said, "Yes, this is hard work. We take Eliza very seriously. Almost every day we see a new change in her. We keep records of every stage."

"She fills up our lives," Higgins added. "We're always teaching Eliza."

"Always dressing Eliza," Pickering chimed in.

"Always inventing new Elizas," Higgins continued.

Higgins and Pickering were so excited about their experiment that they spoke at the same time. Pickering assured Mrs. Higgins that Eliza was a genius and that she played the piano very beautifully, even though she had never touched a piano two months ago. Higgins added that Eliza had a very quick ear and could pick up any dialect. Pickering told about the classical concerts they had taken her to.

Overwhelmed by the chatter, Mrs. Higgins put her fingers in her ears

to block the noise. "Please hush," she scolded.

"I beg your pardon," Pickering apologized, looking at the floor.

"When Pickering shouts, nobody can get a word in," Higgins said.

"I cannot believe how two intelligent men can be so stupid. Don't you fools realize that when Eliza walked into your home, something else came with her—a problem?" Mrs. Higgins asked.

"Oh, you mean the problem of passing her off as a lady," Pickering said.

"I'll solve that problem," Higgins

said. "I've half solved it already."

"No, you two stupid male creatures," Mrs. Higgins replied. "I am talking about the problem of what to do with her when you are done."

"That won't be a problem," Higgins said. "She can go her own way with all of the advantages I have given her."

Mrs. Higgins said that it wasn't as simple as that. When Pickering and Higgins were done with Eliza, she would have the manners and habits that disqualify a fine lady from working. But Eliza wouldn't have the income of a fine lady. How would she live?

"We'll find her some light employment," Higgins said.

"She's happy enough," Pickering assured her. "Don't worry about her."

"Mother, you are worrying needlessly. In any case, there's no use worrying about it now," said Higgins. "What's done is done." He kissed his mother good-bye and headed toward the door with Pickering.

Pickering hesitated for a moment. Then he said, "It's been lovely to see you. Good-bye, dear lady. We'll do what's right."

As they were leaving, Pickering and Higgins discussed taking Eliza to see one of Shakespeare's plays. They thought that her reaction and remarks would be amusing. They laughed as they walked down the stairs.

Mrs. Higgins sighed. She sat down at her writing table to write a letter. After a few minutes she threw down

the pen.

She wondered how she could have raised someone so insensitive to the consequences of his words and actions. The truth was that Mrs. Higgins liked Eliza and didn't want the girl to be hurt by her son. After the experiment was over, Mrs. Higgins knew that Eliza would be left out in the cold, with no place where she felt comfortable. She had lost her old place among the poor in Drury Lane, and most likely she would never feel completely comfortable in fashionable society.

"Oh, men, men, men!" Mrs. Higgins exclaimed in exasperation.

CHAPTER 11

Eliza Passes the Test

It was clear after their visit to Mrs. Higgins's home that Eliza was not ready to pass as a duchess. But Higgins worked tirelessly with her for four more months. Finally, the day arrived for Eliza to be put to the test.

Higgins and Pickering took Eliza to a grand reception at the embassy in London. A long red carpet stretched from the entrance of the embassy all the way to the curb. A small crowd of people gathered to watch all of the guests arrive.

Pickering, dressed in his finest

clothes, with all of his medals hanging from his jacket, helped Eliza out of their limousine. Eliza was wearing her opera cloak, an evening gown, and diamond jewelry. Higgins was the last one out of the car. They walked into the embassy together.

Pickering and Higgins were checking their coats, when the man in front of them on line turned around and nearly bumped into them. The man was young and important looking, and had an extremely hairy face. He recognized Higgins immediately.

"Don't you remember me?" the man asked as he hugged Higgins.

"No, I am afraid I do not," Higgins said. "Who on earth are you?"

"I am Nepommuck, your very first student," the man said. "The last time I saw you I was just a boy. I made your name famous throughout Europe."

"What are you doing here with these important people?" Higgins asked.

"I am an interpreter," explained Nepommuck. "I speak more than thirty languages. They cannot do without me at these international parties. You can place any man in England by his voice. But I can place any man in Europe."

One of the servants came running down the grand staircase. He informed Nepommuck that he was needed upstairs. The ambassador's wife was having a hard time understanding a Greek gentleman who was at the party.

Nepommuck told Higgins that the Greek diplomat in question understood

English perfectly, but pretended not to, and he kept his secret for him—for a very handsome fee.

After Nepommuck went upstairs, Pickering asked, "Do you think this man is expert enough to figure out Eliza and blackmail us?"

"We'll have to wait and see," Higgins replied. "If he is, I'll lose my bet." As he said this, Eliza rejoined them.

"Are you ready, Eliza?" Pickering asked. "I am quite nervous."

"I am not nervous," Eliza said. "I have done this flawlessly in my dreams many times."

When they entered the ballroom, they were greeted by the ambassador, his wife, and Nepommuck.

"How do you do?" Eliza said in perfect English.

The ambassador's wife commented to Pickering that Eliza was lovely and would cause quite a sensation at the party. Then, secretly, she ordered Nepommuck to find out all about Eliza.

Eliza entered the ballroom with the reception already in full swing. As she walked through the room, people stopped to stare at her—her beautiful dress, her jewels, and her regal bearing.

The ambassador's wife asked Higgins to tell her all about Eliza. No woman had caused such a stir in a long time. As they were talking, Nepommuck came running up to them.

"I have found out that the Doolittle woman is a fraud," he said. "She must be a foreigner. She speaks English much too perfectly. Only someone from another country who has just learned the language speaks that properly."

"Where do you think she is from?" asked the ambassador's wife.

"I believe she is from Hungary, like myself," said Nepommuck. "I spoke to her in Hungarian and she asked me to speak only in English because she did not understand French. Quite a clever girl! She must be royalty. I believe she is a princess."

The ambassador's wife asked Higgins for his opinion.

"I believe she is an ordinary English girl taken out of the gutter and taught to speak by an expert."

"I don't think you could be right, Professor Higgins," said the ambassador's wife, shaking her head. "I agree with Nepommuck. She must be a princess, at least."

Higgins walked away from the group to join Pickering. Shortly after that, Eliza joined them.

"I don't think I can take much more," Eliza reported. "Everyone keeps staring at me. I am sorry if I have lost your bet. I have done my best, but nothing can make me the same as these people."

"Oh, Eliza," Higgins said. "You have not lost. You have won my bet for me ten times over! Let's leave. I have had enough of chattering with these fools."

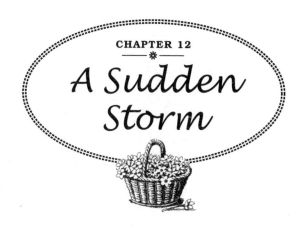

CHAPTER 12
A Sudden Storm

Higgins, Eliza, and Pickering returned home from the party a little after midnight.

Higgins went upstairs. He called to Pickering, "Lock up, will you Pick? We won't be going out again."

"I'll tell Mrs. Pearce to go to bed," replied Pickering. "We won't be needing anything more tonight."

Eliza opened the door and walked into the laboratory. She was still wearing her beautiful evening clothes. She turned on the light and placed her fan, flowers, and other accessories down on the piano. She was very tired. She sat down, looking very sad.

Just then Higgins, still in his evening wear, entered the room. He took off his coat and hat and flung them on the newspaper stand. He threw himself down onto the easy chair. Pickering entered the room, too.

Pickering said, "Mrs. Pearce will be quite angry if we leave all of our things lying about like this."

"Oh, just throw everything over the banister," Higgins replied. "She'll find it in the morning and put it all away.

She'll think we were too tired to put everything away when we came in." Pickering took the coats into the hall to hang them over the banister.

"I wonder where on earth my slippers are," said Higgins.

Eliza looked at him darkly and left the room. Higgins didn't even notice. A few moments later, she returned with Higgins's slippers in her hand. She placed them on the carpet in front of their owner and sat back down in her seat without saying a word.

Higgins yawned. Then he said, "What an evening!" He began to untie his shoelaces when he noticed that the slippers were in front of him. "Oh, there they are," he said.

Pickering came back into the room. "I'm tired," he said. "It's been a long day! But you've won your bet, Higgins. Eliza did the trick, didn't she?"

"I'm just glad that it's all over," Higgins said. Eliza shuddered when he said this, but neither of the men noticed her reaction.

"I was so nervous at the garden party," Pickering said. "Weren't you? Eliza didn't seem the least bit nervous, though."

"I knew she'd be all right," Higgins said. "This job has been a strain. At first, it was interesting. But after the first few weeks, I got very sick of the whole thing. The whole thing has been a bore," he said, yawning.

"Oh, the party was quite exciting, you must admit," Pickering said.

"Maybe for the first three minutes," Higgins replied. "But it's all done now. I can go to bed at last without dreading tomorrow."

"I think I shall turn in, too," Pickering said as he left the room.

Higgins followed him out of the room. Over his shoulder, he called out to Eliza to turn out the lights and to tell Mrs. Pearce that he would have tea in the morning, not coffee.

Eliza tried to control herself as she walked across the room to turn out the lights. But by the time she reached the lamp, she was ready to scream. She sat down in Higgins's chair and grabbed the arms tightly. Finally, she could no longer hold her emotions in, and she flung herself on the floor, sobbing.

"Now what have I done with my slippers," Higgins mumbled as he walked back into the room.

Eliza snatched the slippers and hurled them at him, one after the other, with full force. "There are you slippers," she cried. "Take your slippers and may you never have a day's luck with them."

"What on earth is wrong?" asked Higgins, astounded. "Get up." He pulled Eliza up off of the floor.

"Nothing's wrong with *you*," she cried. "I've won your bet for you, haven't I? That's all you care about. I don't matter to you, do I?"

"*You* won my bet?" Higgins asked.

"I'd like to thrash you, you selfish brute," Eliza said. "Why didn't you just leave me in the gutter? Now that it's all over, you'll probably throw me back there, won't you?"

"Sit down and be quiet," Higgins ordered, looking at her intently.

"What's to become of me?" Eliza cried, her eyes full of fear.

"How am I supposed to know what's to become of you?" Higgins asked. "What does that matter to me?"

"You don't care about me," Eliza said. "I'm nothing to you. Them slippers mean more to you."

"Those slippers," Higgins corrected.

Eliza gave up, hopeless and crushed. Higgins was a bit uneasy. He asked Eliza if she had anything to complain about regarding her treatment at his house. Had anyone treated her badly? Eliza admitted that no one had.

"Go to bed like a good girl and sleep

it off," Higgins said. "Now you are free to do what you like."

"What am I fit for?" Eliza asked. "What have you left me fit for? Where am I to go? What am I to do? What's to become of me?"

Higgins paced the room, rattling the contents of his pockets. He tried to brush off Eliza's comments as though they were trivial. "Is that all you're worried about?" he asked. "You're pleasant to look at sometimes. You might marry. Not all men are confirmed bachelors like Pickering and I."

Eliza just stared at him, speechless. Higgins simply sat back and ate an apple without a care in the world.

"My mother might be able to find you a chap," Higgins finally said, looking relieved at the thought.

"I sold flowers, not myself," Eliza said coldly. "You've made me a lady. Now I am not fit to sell anything. I wish you'd left me where you found me."

"What about your idea of a flower shop?" Higgins offered. "Pickering could set you up. He has lots of money. You'll be all right." He got up and headed out of the room.

"Do my clothes belong to me or to Colonel Pickering, sir?" Eliza asked.

Higgins was surprised that Eliza had called him "sir." "What use would they be to Pickering?" Higgins asked.

"He might want them for the next girl you experiment on," said Eliza.

"Is that what you think of us?"
Higgins asked. "Why are you bothering
about this in the middle of the night?"

"I want to know what I can take with
me," Eliza replied forcefully. "I don't want
to be accused of stealing after I leave."

"You may take the whole houseful
with you, if you like," Higgins said.
"Does that satisfy you?"

Eliza knew that she had hurt his
feelings, and she was glad. She took
off her jewels, handed them to Higgins,
and asked him to take them to his
room. She said she didn't want to risk
them being missing.

He snatched the jewels from her and
jammed them into his pocket. Eliza felt
as though she had gotten him back, in
a small way.

"You have caused me to lose my
temper," Higgins said. "I won't have any
more of this. I am going to bed. And
you should do the same."

"Leave a note for Mrs. Pearce," Eliza

said. "She won't be told about your morning tea by me!"

"I am angry at myself for spending so much time and hard-earned knowledge on a heartless guttersnipe like you," Higgins said calmly. He slammed the door as he left the room.

Eliza wiped the tears from her eyes and smiled at the thought of making Higgins furious. Then she clenched her fists and stormed up the stairs.

CHAPTER 13
Freddy and Eliza

Eliza changed into a casual dress and put on her hat and walking shoes, determined to put her experience with the ruthless Henry Higgins behind her. She was very careful to put her fancy clothes neatly into her closet. She took a last look at herself in the mirror and stuck out her tongue at her reflection.

Then Eliza ran out of the house and slammed the door. To her great surprise, she found Freddy Eynsford Hill standing outside the house, staring up at her window.

"What on earth are you doing here?" she asked him.

"Don't laugh at me," said Freddy. "I spend most of my nights out here, waiting to catch a glimpse of you."

Eliza broke down. "You don't think I am a heartless guttersnipe, do you?" she asked.

"Of course not!" said Freddy. "How can you imagine such a thing? You are so lovely and dear." Unable to control his emotions any longer, he kissed Eliza. A policeman walked by and, embarrassed at their display, Freddy and Eliza ran

off.

When they finally stopped running, Freddy asked Eliza where she was going at such a late hour. Eliza told him that she was going down to the river to think about her life.

"What's wrong?" Freddy asked.

"It doesn't matter now, I suppose," Eliza replied thoughtfully. "You love me, and as long as someone loves me, I guess nothing is wrong."

Eliza didn't know what to do. She was very confused. But if Freddy loved her, she thought, perhaps that was her way out of her situation. She wouldn't have to worry about her future or what she was going to do next. But, did she love Freddy in return?

Eliza wasn't thinking very clearly. She decided to drive around in a taxi with Freddy all night. Then she would call on Mrs. Higgins in the morning and ask for her help and advice.

CHAPTER 14
Doolittle's News

The next day, Mrs. Higgins was sitting at her writing table when her parlor maid came into the room to announce guests. "Mr. Henry is downstairs with Colonel Pickering," she said.

"Show them up," Mrs. Higgins replied briskly.

"I thought I'd better tell you that they're using the telephone to call the police," the parlor maid said.

"I would be more surprised if you had told me that Mr. Henry wasn't agitated about something," Mrs. Higgins said. "I suppose he's lost something and is

reporting it."

She told her maid to go upstairs to let Eliza know that Higgins and Pickering were there and not to come down until she was called for. With nowhere else to go, Eliza had gone to Mrs. Higgins's house that morning, as she had planned.

Just then, Higgins burst into the room in a state of panic. "Eliza's run away," he said to his mother.

"You must have frightened her," Mrs. Higgins said calmly.

"Nonsense!" yelled Higgins. "I left her in the laboratory last night and instead of going to bed, she left. What am I to do?"

"The girl has a perfect right to leave if she chooses," said Mrs. Higgins.

Higgins wandered distractedly across the room. "But I can't find anything and I can't remember my appointments," he complained.

Pickering came into the room, said hello to Mrs. Higgins, and sat down.

"What did the inspector say?" Higgins

demanded. "Did you offer a reward for Eliza?"

Mrs. Higgins was utterly amazed. "Do you mean to say you've set the police after Eliza, as though she were a thief or a lost umbrella? Really!"

Higgins and Pickering explained that they wanted to find her and didn't know how else to do so. The conversation was interrupted by the parlor maid, who came in to tell Higgins that there was a gentleman to see him. He had been sent there from Wimpole Street.

"Who is it?" asked Higgins.

"A Mr. Doolittle," answered the maid.

"Not the old dustman," mumbled Higgins.

"Oh, no, sir," said the maid. "This Mr. Doolittle is a gentleman."

Higgins thought that it was another of Eliza's relatives there to bribe him, just like her father had. He ordered the maid to show the man up.

It *was* Eliza's father. He was now

respectably dressed in a fashionable coat and gray trousers. He also wore fancy shoes and a silk top hat. There was a fresh flower in his buttonhole.

"Do you see the way I am dressed?" asked Doolittle. "You done this to me, Higgins. My life is no longer my own."

"Has Eliza been buying you clothes?" asked Higgins.

Doolittle explained that he had bought his new clothes. Higgins, apparently, had written a letter to a friend in America, who happened to head the Moral Reform

Society. Jokingly, Higgins had told his friend that Doolittle was the most moral person in all of England. But his friend had believed Higgins, and when he died, he left Doolittle three thousand pounds a year. In return, he had requested that Doolittle give six lectures a year about morality!

But Doolittle did not want to be a gentleman. "When I was poor, I was free," he said. "A year ago, nobody wanted anything to do with me. Now everyone wants to see me all of the time!"

"Well, if it upsets you so," Mrs. Higgins

said, "don't accept it."

"I don't have much of a choice," Doolittle said. "It's either the money or the workhouse, and I don't want to spend the rest of my life working."

"Well, at least this solves the problem of Eliza's future," Mrs. Higgins said. "You can provide for her now."

"Nonsense," Higgins cried. "She belongs to me. I paid him five pounds for her. Have you taken her?"

"Eliza is upstairs," Mrs. Higgins revealed.

Immediately Henry jumped up to get Eliza. But his mother insisted that he sit down and listen to her. Eliza had told Mrs. Higgins about the brutal way he had treated her. Mrs. Higgins explained that Eliza had become attached to Higgins and Pickering. Eliza had done a wonderful job of winning Higgins his bet, and he had never thanked her or complimented her.

"She knew how I felt," said Higgins

defensively. "I didn't have to say anything to her."

"Perhaps we were inconsiderate," Pickering conceded. "Is she very angry?"

"She won't go back to Wimpole Street," Mrs. Higgins said. "But she's willing to let bygones be bygones. If you promise to behave yourself, Henry, I'll ask her to come down."

"Very well," Higgins said.

Mrs. Higgins turned to Doolittle and asked him to wait on the balcony. She did not want Eliza to be shocked by his

presence. "Please ask Eliza to join us," she said to the maid. "Tell her that my son and Colonel Pickering have come and would like a word with her."

The parlor maid left to do as she was instructed, while Higgins and Pickering stood in a tense silence, waiting for their star pupil.

"Where on earth is that girl? Are we to wait here all day?" asked Higgins impatiently.

As he was complaining, Eliza came into the room. She seemed very confident and very much at home. "How do you do, Professor Higgins? Are you quite well?" she asked.

Higgins was too shocked to answer at first. Then he said, "Don't play games with me, young lady. Get up and come home this instant."

"How could any woman resist such an invitation," Mrs. Higgins said.

But Eliza just picked up some needlework, sat down, and began to stitch, ignoring Higgins's outburst.

"I created this thing out of the squashed cabbage leaves of Covent Garden," Higgins said. "Now she pretends to play the fine lady with me!"

"Will you drop me altogether now that the experiment is over?" Eliza asked Pickering, ignoring Higgins completely.

"Oh, no," Pickering said, "you mustn't think that way."

"I owe so much to you," Eliza continued, "that I would be very unhappy if you forgot about me."

"That's very kind of you," Pickering replied, smiling.

"It was from you that I learned nice manners," Eliza said. "Professor Higgins didn't set a very good example in that department. I never would have known how gentlemen and ladies behaved if you hadn't been around."

"He taught you how to speak properly," said Pickering.

"That's his profession," Eliza replied. "My real education began the moment you called me Miss Doolittle. That was the beginning of self-respect for me. You never took your boots off in the dining room, or did any of the rude things that Professor Higgins did."

"Thank you, Miss Doolittle," Pickering said. "But Henry doesn't mean any disrespect. It's just his way."

"Colonel Pickering, I would like you to call me Eliza from now on," said Eliza, "and Professor Higgins should call me Miss Doolittle."

"Should I?" Higgins asked, raising his eyebrows.

"Stand up for yourself, Eliza!" laughed Pickering. "It will do him good."

"I can't go back to my old ways now," Eliza said. "I have forgotten my old way of speaking."

"Eliza, will you forgive Henry and come back to Wimpole Street?" Pickering asked hopefully.

"Forgive! Let her go and find out how lost she is without us," said Higgins spitefully. "You'll see. She'll be back in the gutter in a week."

By that time, Eliza's father had grown tired of standing on the balcony. He came into the room silently and walked up behind Eliza. When he touched her shoulder, Eliza dropped her needlework and let out a loud "Ah-ah-ow-ow-ee!" She was surprised at the way her father was dressed.

"Aha!" Higgins yelled in triumph. "I knew she would go back to her old

habits and way of speaking!"

"Have you swindled a millionaire?" Eliza asked her father.

"I'll explain later," Doolittle said. "I've come to tell you that I am getting married today. And I want you to come to the wedding."

"You're going to marry that common woman?" asked Eliza.

"It would be the right thing to do," Pickering said. "You should go to the wedding, Eliza. Make the best of it." He squeezed her elbow gently.

"If Colonel Pickering thinks it best, I will go," Eliza said, although she didn't really want to.

"I'm nervous," said Doolittle. "It would make me feel better if you all came."

Everyone agreed to go to Doolittle's wedding to offer him support. Mrs. Higgins left the room to arrange for the carriage. Pickering and Doolittle also left the room to get ready. That left Eliza and Higgins alone together.

CHAPTER 16
Farewell, Henry Higgins

Eliza walked onto the balcony. She wanted to avoid being alone with Higgins. Higgins followed her, so she came back into the room and ran for the door. But Higgins blocked the door before she had the chance.

"You want me back only to fetch your slippers," Eliza said.

Higgins said, "I haven't said I wanted you back at all. But if you do come back, I'll treat you the same as I always have. My manners are exactly the same as Colonel Pickering's."

"That's not true," Eliza argued. "He

treats a flower girl as if she were a duchess."

"And I treat a duchess as if she were a flower girl," Higgins replied.

"I see," said Eliza. "You treat everyone the same."

"The secret is not having good or bad manners," Higgins said, "but having the same manners for all. The question is not whether I treat you rudely, but whether you ever heard me treat anyone else better."

"I don't care how you treat me or if you swear at me," said Eliza sincerely.

"I just won't be passed over as if I were nothing. I can do without you."

"You never asked yourself, I suppose, if I could do without you," said Higgins. "I can do without anybody. But I shall miss you, Eliza. I have grown accustomed to your voice and face. I rather like them." He sat down next to Eliza on the sofa.

"Well, you have them on your gramophone and in your photos," said Eliza. Looking down, she said, "You do know how to twist a girl's heart."

Higgins explained to Eliza that, although she thought he was a brute, he was not. Getting his slippers and finding his glasses made her a servant. In fact, he thought a woman getting things for a man was disgusting. He had thought much more of Eliza when she had thrown the slippers at him.

"Why did you teach me all of this if you didn't care for me?" Eliza asked.

"It was my job," Higgins replied.

"Understand that I go about my business and do my work without caring what happens to either of us."

"Then what am I to come back for?" Eliza asked.

"For the fun of it," Higgins replied.

"You might throw me out tomorrow if I don't do everything you want me to," Eliza said.

"Yes," Higgins replied, "and you might walk out tomorrow if I don't do everything you want me to."

"If only I could go back to my flower basket and my old life," Eliza said. "Why did I let you take my independence from me?"

"I'll adopt you as my daughter, or you can get Colonel Pickering to marry you," Higgins half-joked.

"That's not what I want," Eliza said. "If I wanted that, I could turn to Freddy Eynsford Hill. He writes me lots of love letters."

This made Higgins angry. He didn't

think Freddy was good enough for Eliza. But Eliza disagreed. She thought Freddy had every right to love her if he wanted to.

"You shouldn't encourage him," Higgins said. "He's a fool. Can he make anything of you?"

"Maybe I could make something of him," Eliza replied. "But I don't want us to make anything out of each other. I just want to be natural."

"So, you want me to be as infatuated with you as Freddy is?" asked Higgins.

"No, I don't," Eliza said. "I just want a little kindness. I know I'm common, but I'm not dirt under your feet. I didn't take part in your experiment for the clothes and jewels. I came to care for you as a friend."

"That's how I feel, too," Higgins said. "But I will never be a kind, unselfish person. Go marry some sentimental fool. If you can't appreciate what you've got, go get what you can appreciate."

Eliza said, "You know you are a bully, and you know I can't go back to the gutter, and you know I have no real friends in the world except for you and the colonel. But don't think I have nowhere to go. I'll marry Freddy as soon as he is able to support me."

"But you are now fit to marry someone with a good position," Higgins argued. "I won't have my masterpiece thrown away on Freddy Eynsford Hill."

"I'll show you that I can be independent," said a determined Eliza. "I can become a teacher. I'll advertise in the papers that your duchess is merely a flower girl you taught, and that she can teach anyone to be a duchess in the same amount of time."

"You disrespectful girl, you," Higgins shouted. "But I guess it's better than you sniveling. Better than fetching slippers, isn't it? By George, I said I'd make a woman of you, and I have." He smiled triumphantly.

"It figures that you would make up with me now that I am not afraid of you," Eliza said.

"Yes, now you're a tower of strength," Higgins said. "You, Pickering, and I will be three silly old bachelors instead of two men and a silly girl."

Mrs. Higgins came back to tell Eliza that the carriage was ready to take them to Doolittle's wedding. Eliza instantly became cool and elegant again. She asked whether Higgins was coming, and his mother forbade it since she didn't think that Higgins could behave himself properly in the church.

"Then I shall not see you again, Professor," Eliza said. "Good-bye."

Higgins ignored the remark. He believed that Eliza would indeed be returning to Wimpole Street soon.

"By the way, Eliza," Higgins said, "buy me a tie and a pair of gloves, size eight, to match that new suit of mine. You may choose the color."

"Size eight is too small for you," Eliza replied. "And you have three new ties in your closet. What you will do without me, I do not know." With that, she swept out of the room.

Higgins was quite sure he knew Eliza better than she thought. "Going to marry Freddy! Ha!" said Higgins and he roared with laughter.

About the Author

George Bernard Shaw was born in Dublin, Ireland, in 1856. At the age of twenty, Shaw moved to London, England, with his mother and sister. For two years, he worked as a junior clerk to support his family. He educated himself by studying at the British Museum.

Shaw began writing novels and eventually became an accomplished drama and music critic. In 1898, he began to write plays. An advocate of women's rights and social equality, Shaw explored his views in his work. His masterpieces include *Caesar and Cleopatra*, *Man and Superman*, *Arms and the Man*, and *Pygmalion*.

In 1950, Shaw died at Ayot St. Lawrence, Hertfordshire, England, at the age of ninety-four. In 1964, *My Fair Lady*, a film based on *Pygmalion*, was released. Both Shaw's play and the movie are now considered to be classics.